Dedication: To "Buttonhill" and its former stewards, (G.&T. Hoyt, J. Burnett, E.&P. Walker) whose hands, imagination and love made that place a sanctuary. And most of all, with love to my husband Jack, for the four idyllic years we spent there.

Copyright ©1999 by Redenta Soprano
All rights reserved. No part of this book may be reproduced in any form or by any electronic or mechanical means, including information storage and retrieval systems, without permission in writing from the publisher, except by a reviewer who may quote brief passages in a review.

Soprano, Redenta
Philosophical Nature A Book of Haiku Poetry
Summary: A collection of Haiku Poetry illustrated in black and white by the author.

ISBN: 0-9674603-0-1

Library of Congress Card Catalog Number
99-96003

Special Edition CeReS Press, Stamford, CT ~ USA

Philosophical Nature

A Book of Haiku Poetry
by Redenta Soprano

"When Nature whispers
Only those with quiet hearts
Can truly listen."

Redenta Soprano

©1999

CeRes press

About the Book

For a short time my husband and I had the privilege of living in Redding, Connecticut. The home in which we resided had been loved and tended by its three previous owners from the day it was built. Every corner of the house, mossy nook, tree and ledge in the garden emanated the love and care that had been infused into the property over the years.

At times, the responsibility of the grounds-keeping seemed like a daunting regimen. Yet with simple relaxation into the routine of weeding the perennial garden, raking leaves or quietly sweeping the moss, the poetry would come unaided and intact. It was as though in that sanctified space Nature Herself would do the dictating.

Haiku is an effective way of crystallizing thoughts into a moment in time. Far better than a diary, the instant and place each poem was conceived can clearly be re-collected.

The illustrations are rendered in scratchboard and pen and ink. The rectangular motif in each of the drawings loosely reflects the structured format of the haiku poem.

About Haiku Poetry

The haiku is a disciplined form of Japanese poetry that is comprised of three lines. Each line contains 5, 7 and 5 syllables respectively, that add up to a total of 17 syllables per poem.

Traditionally the brief words describe a particular time or season that simultaneously evoke a mood of transcendental awareness.

From the 15th through 17th Centuries in Japan, Haiku was a popular form of self-expression and was often composed by itinerant Zen Buddhist monks.

Garden

Sliding a two-step
to my rake's scratchy rhythm
agrarian dance

Stooping to pick sticks
on such a blustery day
wind lusts for my hat

Soiled garden gloves
curved palms and tattered fingers
hands' caricatures

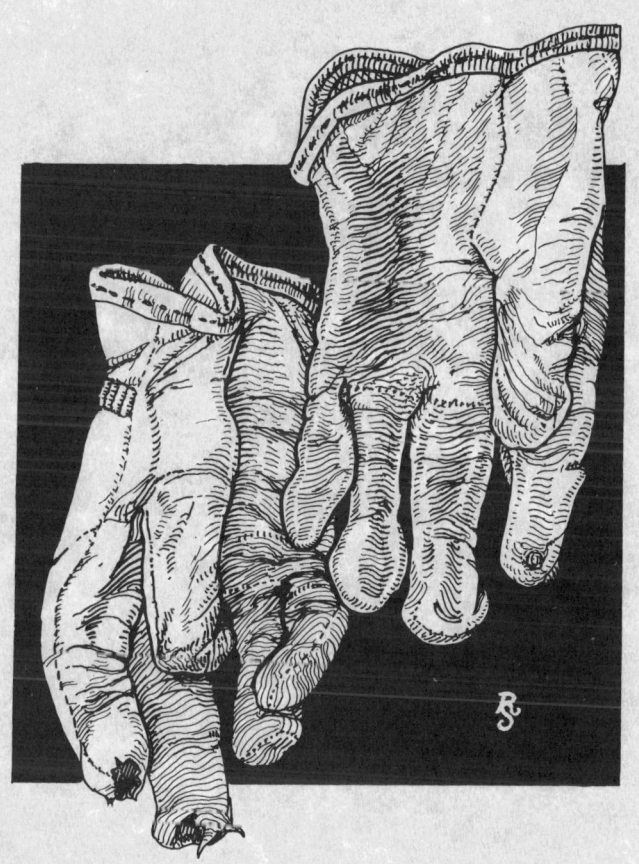

What a stunning leek!
green-striped suit and tasseled foot
the soup's honored guest

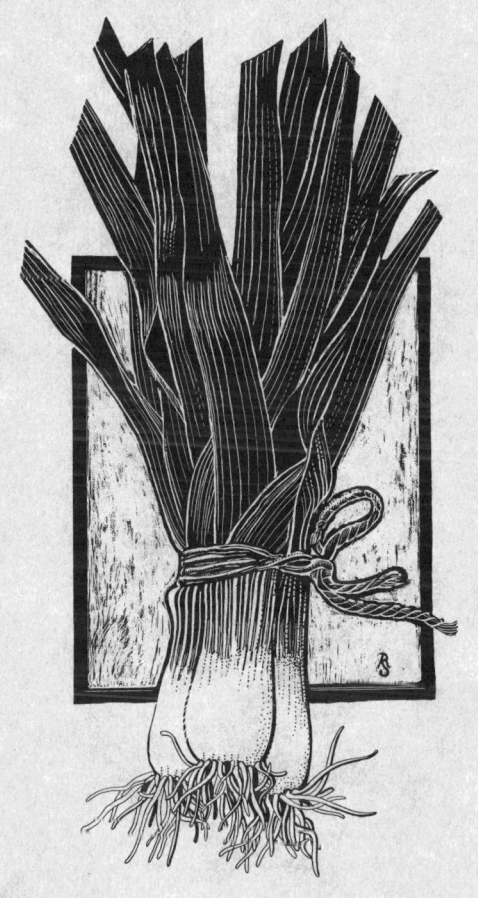

A sip of water
at its dry root, with fragrance
sweet rose rewards me

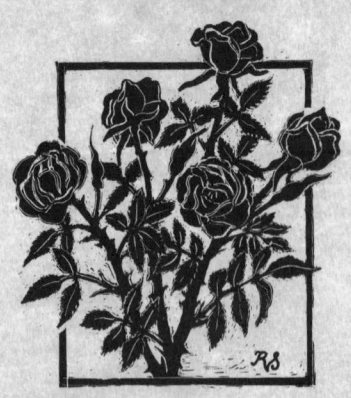

Many

The ten thousand things
are they all so commonplace?
No. Miraculous!

Why so fussy cat?
Cold rain out the front door
quite the same out the back!

Our two green jackets
hanging outside to dry
sway gently in tandem

From his cell's doorway
monk offers a crust of bread
to his bold friend, Crow

Beneath melting snow
soft squeaks and rustling, vole waits,
impatient for spring

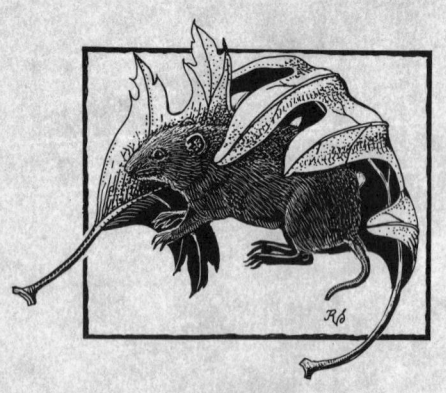

Seasons

Aloft one-by-one
turning in the autumn breeze
milkweed dervishes

Woolly bear passing
arrayed in orange and black
exits October

Treasured in a vase
even as their color fades
these last summer blooms

Bathed in thin, cold light
its bent head brown and withered
winter solstice rose

Who's still blooming here
this last dark month of the year?
one blue-eyed myrtle

Night and Day

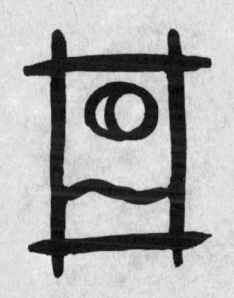

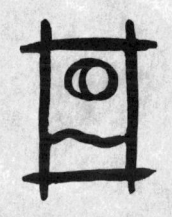

Window frames of light
move silent across my desk
afternoon passing

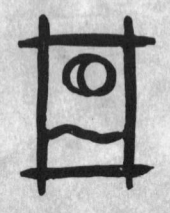

New moon at sunset
one crystalline fingernail
from the Divine Hand

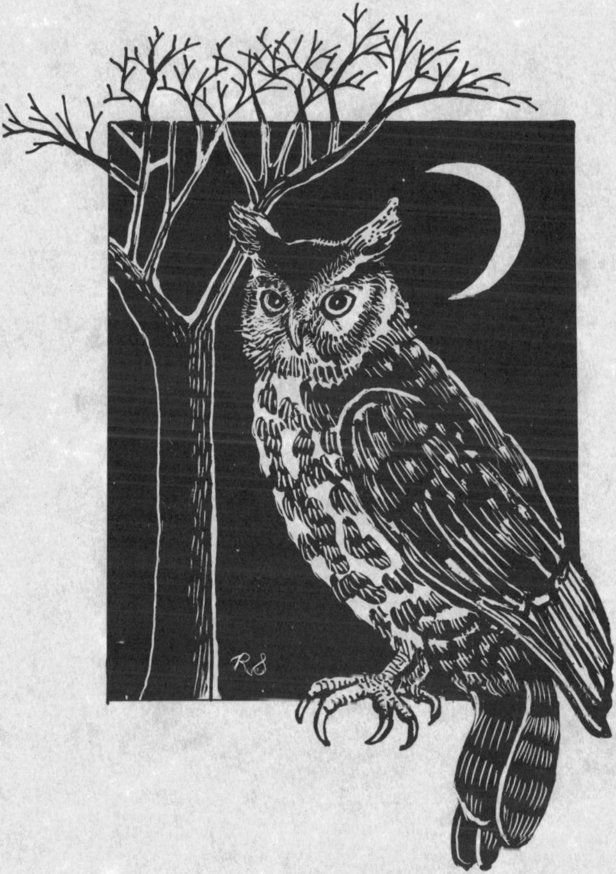

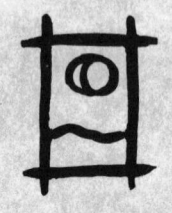

Where has this day gone?
Minutes flowed from my pen tip
counted out in words

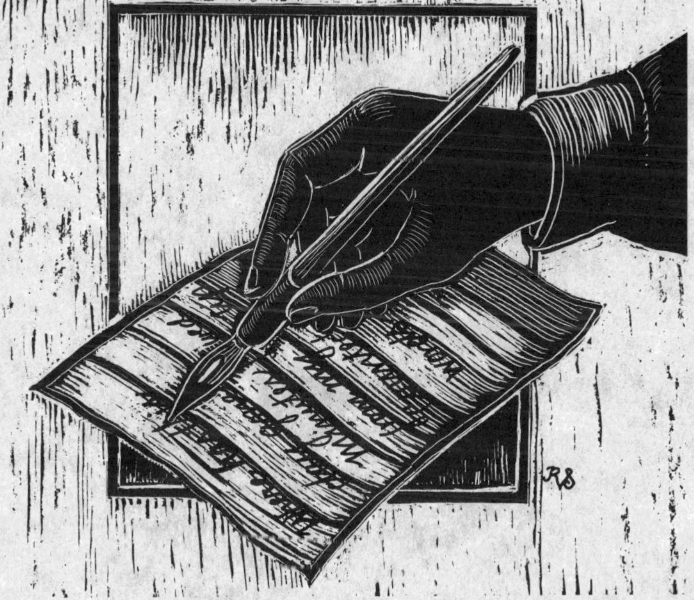

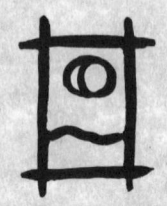

Rising through dark clouds
single, gold half-lidded eye
introspective moon

The Path

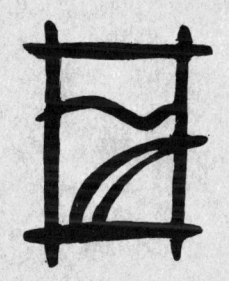

Thought is our fabric
when You spin the threads of words
i will stitch love notes

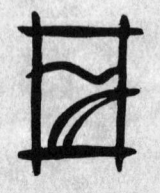

This hot angry world
relief only to gaze on
the faces of saints

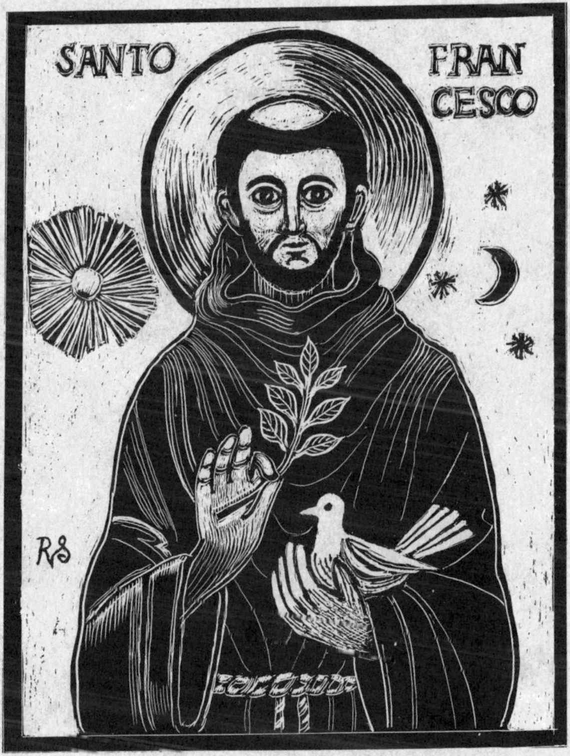
SANTO
FRAN
CESCO
RS

Day by passing day
Your astonishing beauty
feeds my secret flame

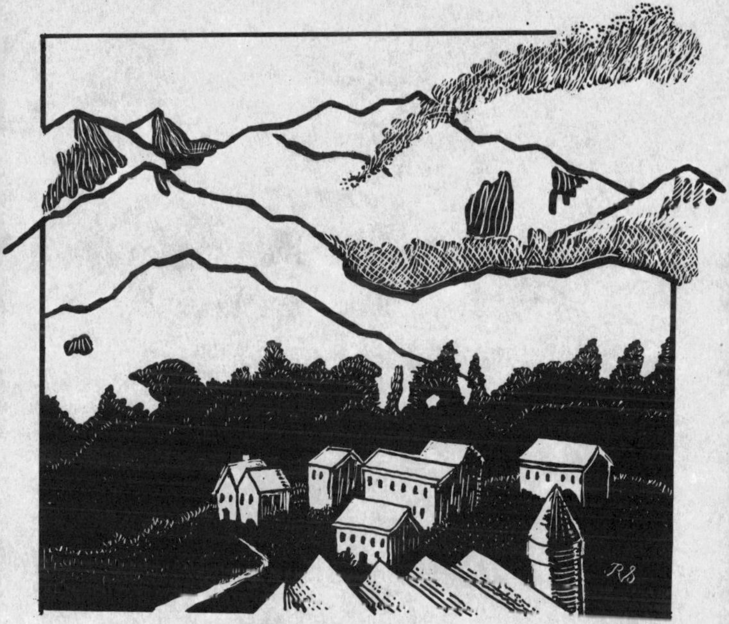

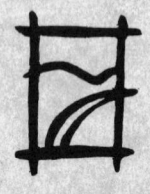

Lord, You've given us
flowers, birds and beasts as kin
in this vast Alone

47

What are God's feet like?
In great fields of stars they dance
churning forth the Light!

About the Author/Artist

"Large eyes, thin mouth,
much to see and contemplate
so few words to say"

Growing up in the country, in a family where Nature was revered with almost a religious zeal, Redenta knew from an early age that illustrating natural subjects would be her calling.

For many years she has worked as a freelance artist specializing in botanical subjects. She also teaches, writes and is presently living with her husband John Kern and cat "Kili" somewhere between Florida and Connecticut.